Library of Congress Cataloging-in-Publication Data

Watts, Barrie.
   Potato.

   (Stopwatch books)
   Originally published: London : A & C Black, c1987.
   Summary: Describes in simple terms and illustrations
how the potato develops from a shoot to a plant with
the edible parts growing underground.
   1. Potatoes--Juvenile literature.   2. Potatoes--
Development--Juvenile literatue.   [1. Potatoes]
I. Title.   II. Series.
SB211.P8W28   1988   635'.21   87-016702
   ISBN 0-382-09528-6
   ISBN 0-382-09527-8 (lib. bdg.)

Published by A & C Black (Publishers) Limited
35 Bedford Row, London WC1R 4JH

© 1987 Barrie Watts

Adapted and published in the United States in 1988
by Silver Burdett Press, Morristown, New Jersey

Acknowledgements
The artwork is by Helen Senior
The publishers wish to thank Jean Imrie for her help and advise.

Printed in Hong Kong by Dai Nippon Printing Co. Ltd.

Stopwatch books

Potato

Barrie Watts

Silver Burdett Press • Morristown, New Jersey

Here are some potatoes.

Mashed potatoes, boiled potatoes, chips, or fries. There are lots of ways you can eat potatoes.

There are lots of different kinds of potatoes, too.

All these potatoes grew the same way. They grew under the ground in fields and gardens.

This book will tell you how potatoes grow.

The potato grows a shoot.

Look at the skin of this potato.

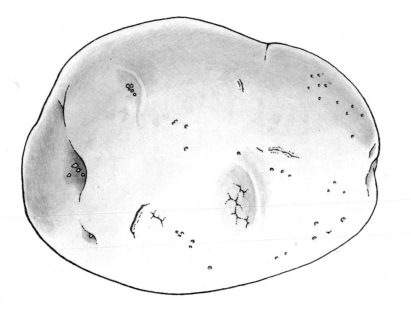

It is not smooth. It has bumps and dents on it.
These bumps and dents are called eyes.
Sometimes shoots may grow out of the eyes.

Look at the big photograph. Tiny shoots have
started to grow out of this eye.

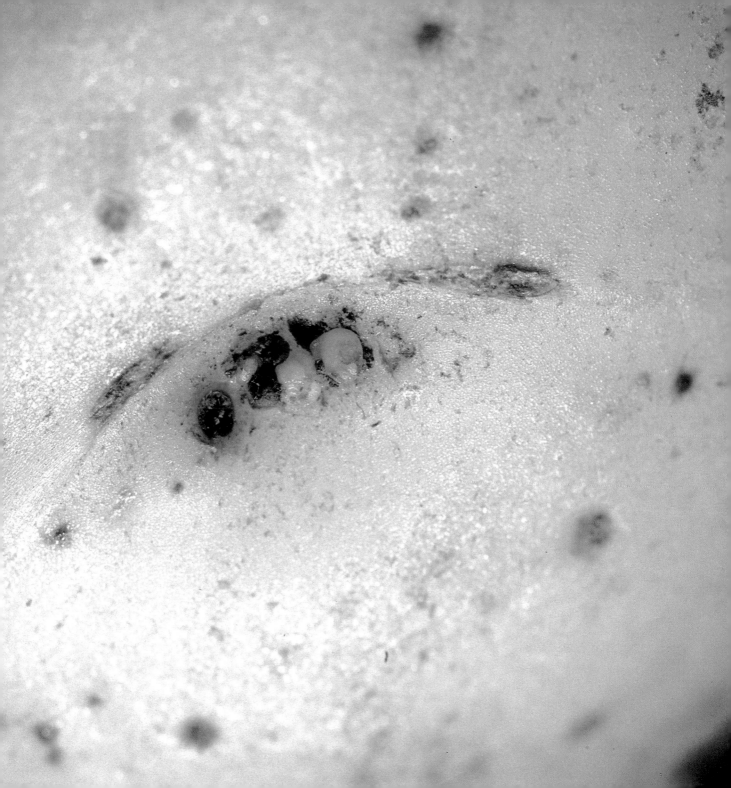

The shoot grows bigger.

This potato has been cut in half.

The skin covers the outside of the potato. The inside contains a supply of food for the young plant.
This food is made of starch.

After about two weeks, one shoot has grown bigger. It has started to grow tiny leaves. The shoot needs food to grow. It uses the food stored in the potato.

Leaves open on the plant.

Each day the shoot grows bigger. It is growing up through the soil toward the light.

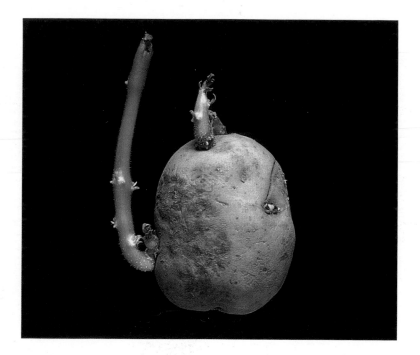

The potato is old and green. More shoots are starting to grow from it. Can you see tiny roots starting to grow?

When a shoot has reached the top of the soil, its leaves begin to unfold. The leaves open up to catch the light. The plant needs light and air to live and grow.

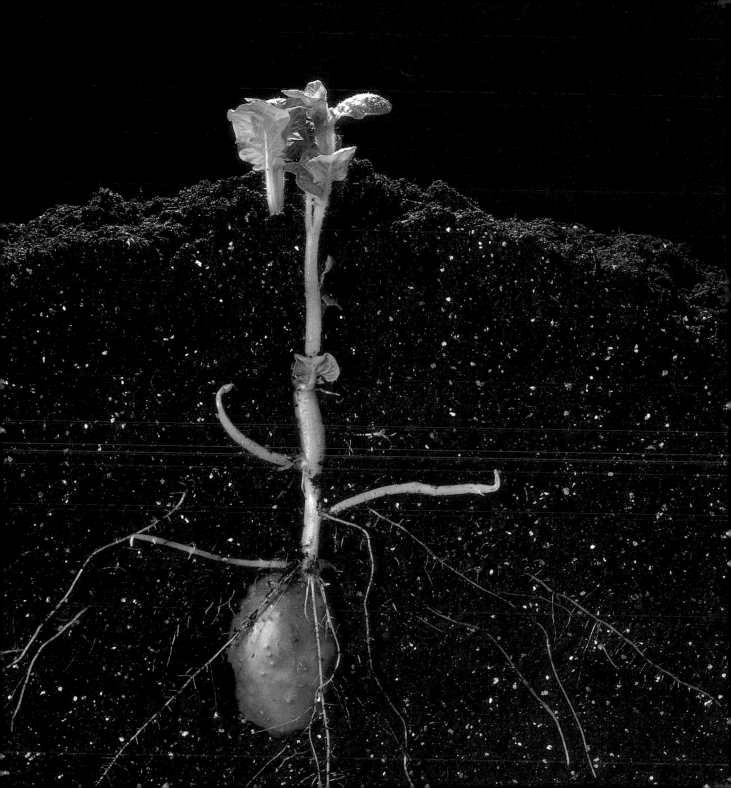

The plant has roots.

The roots of the plant are growing under the ground. They spread out through the soil, like this.

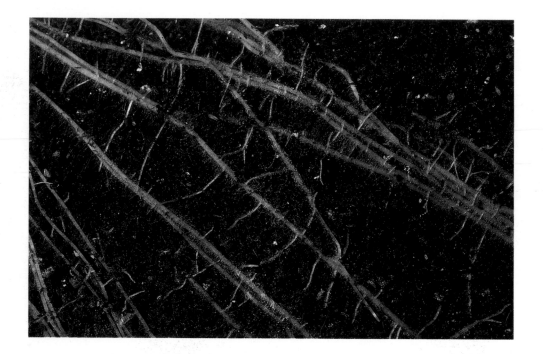

Can you see the tiny hairs on the roots? The hairs take in water and goodness from the soil.

Look at the big photograph. Can you see the potato? It is getting rotten. The plant has used up nearly all the food in the potato. Now it makes its own food.

A tiny potato starts to grow.

The plant uses some of its food. It stores the rest of the food
at the end of special thick stems under the ground.
The food is stored in bumps called tubers.
Each tuber is a tiny potato. It is as big as the top of a match.

Look at the drawing.

Can you see the tiny potatoes starting to grow? They are
too small to eat. Above the ground, the plant has grown
buds. Soon flowers will open.

The potato plant has flowers.

On a sunny day, the flowers open. The middle of each flower is covered with yellow dust, called pollen.

This beetle is eating some pollen.

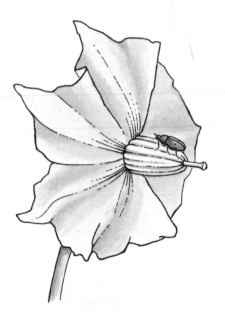

Some of the pollen has brushed onto the beetle's body. When the beetle goes to another flower, some pollen may rub off. If the pollen touches the middle of the flower, a fruit may start to grow.

The potato plant has seeds.

After about eight weeks, the potato plant grows fruit.

These fruits are each about as big as a marble. They are poisonous and you must not eat them.

Look at the big photograph. This fruit has been cut in half. Look at all the seeds inside. If a seed lands on the soil, a tiny potato plant may start to grow.

Under the ground the potato grows bigger.

The potato plant keeps making food. Under the ground, the tiny potatoes are growing bigger. Each one is now about as big as a grape. Look at the drawing.

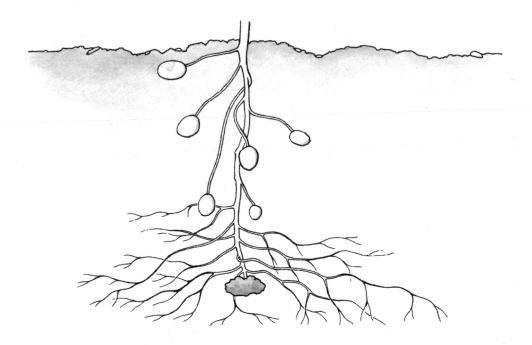

How many small potatoes can you see?

The potatoes must be covered with soil. If light reaches a potato, the potato will turn green. The green bits are poisonous.

The potato is fully grown.

After about twelve weeks, the potato plant has stopped growing.

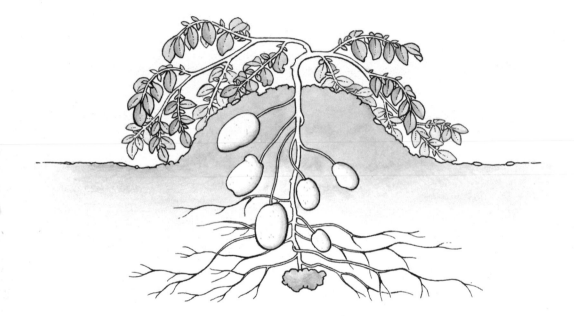

The leaves dry up and die. The plant has stored food in the potatoes.

Look at the photograph. This potato is fully grown.
If no one digs it up, it will grow shoots next spring.
Then new potato plants will grow.

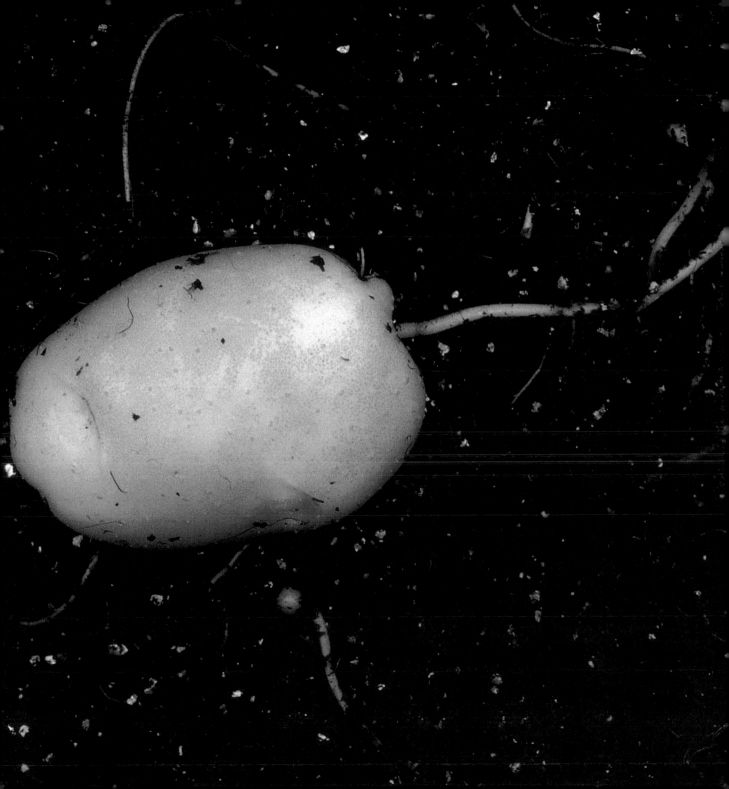

The potato is ready to eat.

This potato has been dug up. It is ready to cook and eat.
How do you like to eat potatoes?

If you do not cook your potato, it may grow a shoot.
Then you can plant it.

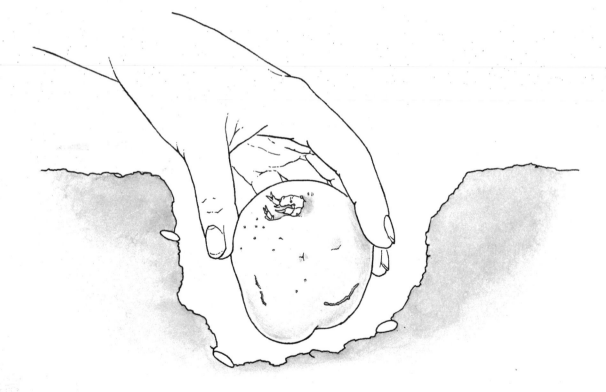

What do you think will happen when you plant the potato?

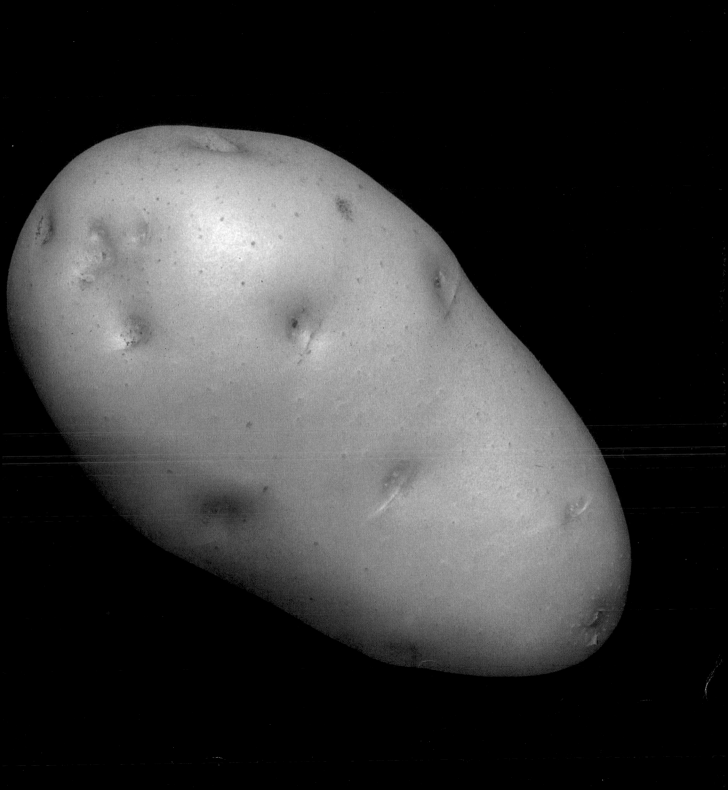

Do you remember how a potato grows?
See if you can tell the story in your own words.
You can use these pictures to help you.

1

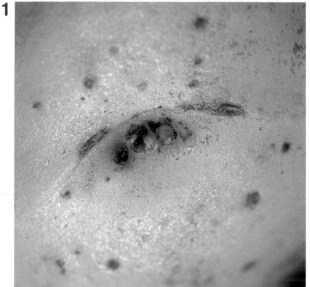

2

4

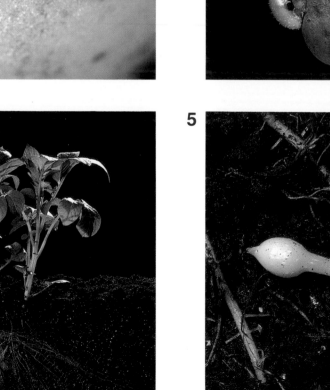

5

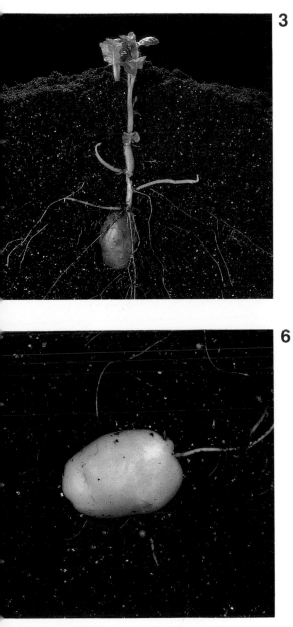

3

6

Index

This index will help you
to find some of the important
words in the book.

a potato on the windowsill and see shoots grow from the eyes.
can plant the potato and watch the shoot grow into a plant.